OMG!
I WROTE A BOOK
...
NOW WHAT?

PUBLISHING OPTIONS
& QUESTIONS TO ASK

JULEE BRAND

ONBRAND BOOKS

an imprint of W. Brand Publishing

NASHVILLE, TENNESSEE

Copyright © 2023 JuLee Brand.

All rights reserved. No part of this publication may be reproduced, distributed or transmitted in any form or by any means, including photocopying, recording, or other electronic or mechanical methods, without the prior written permission of the publisher, except in the case of brief quotations embodied in critical reviews and certain other noncommercial uses permitted by copyright law.

Author has no responsibility for the persistence or accuracy of URLs for external or third-party Internet Websites referred to in this publication and does not guarantee that any content on such Websites is, or will remain, accurate or appropriate.

None of the companies referenced within the book have endorsed the book.

Information in this book is based on the real world publishing industry experience of the author at the time of publishing. Changes in the industry my render some information obsolete.

ONBrand Books is an imprint of W. Brand Publishing

For information contact: j.brand@wbrandpub.com

Cover design: designchik.net

OMG! I Wrote A Book . . . Now What? /JuLee Brand —1st ed.

Paperback ISBN: 978-1-956906-57-8

eBook ISBN:978-1-956906-58-5

CONTENTS

Introduction vii

Chapter 1: Personal Author Goals 1

Chapter 2: Overview of all types of Publishing 5

Chapter 3: The Big Five 9

Chapter 4: Academic/University/Small Presses 13

Chapter 5: Independent Publishers 15

Chapter 6: Self-Publishing / Author-published 21

Chapter 7: Vetting Future Publisher 25

Chapter 8: Other Aspects of Book Publishing 31

Chapter 9: Final Thoughts 37

Resources 39

Acknowledgments 43

About the Author 45

To everyone who has ever written a book and put it aside not knowing what to do next.

INTRODUCTION

WHY YOU NEED THIS BOOK

If you are reading this, you have finished your book but have no idea what to do with it now. Or perhaps you are almost done writing but are an information geek like I am and want to get your plan together so you don't "waste" any time.

Whether you have been writing your story for a decade or the past ten days, the next obvious step for your project is to publish, but with all the choices available, how do you know what the best option for YOU is?

Depending on whom you talk to, you will hear about a wide variety of publishing options. More than likely, you'll also get their bias as to how you should publish. My challenge for you is to take in as much information about publishing as you can or care to digest. And for those who remember Saturday morning cartoons, "The More You Know" is real and will help you navigate your many choices without wasting time or money.

WHY I WROTE THIS BOOK

After years of research and publishing over thirty authors in various ways from traditional, hybrid, and author-publishing (also known as self-publishing), I knew it was time to create a reference guide for writers when I found myself repeating the same information daily in initial discovery calls. By publishing this little handbook, my goal is to be able to save the potential author time by "getting to the verb" or taking action in making their publishing decision.

I was an Art Director at a Big Five publishing company, ran a self-publishing department for a ghostwriting company, and currently have my own boutique hybrid publishing company where I vet authors and publish books that fit our mission. I also help authors self-publish if that is more in line with their goals.

Being a true believer in the adage that it is better to teach a man to fish so he can feed himself, I also know there are many authors who have no interest in "fishing" but do enjoy a good boat ride. Either way, you will find useful information in this book to help you decide your publishing path.

THINGS TO CONSIDER WHEN MAKING YOUR PUBLISHER CHOICE

Before making a choice, the first thing to do is look at the resources in your control: time and money.

While traditional publishing does not require a financial investment by the author, it does require agents, proposals, and a lot of patience. There are more publishing options in which there is an investment of capital, and for that, a budget should be set before talking to publishers. The budget may need to be adjusted later, but this exercise will help establish how serious you are about the publishing process.

The other resource you have control over is the investment of time. It's important to determine how much time in your schedule you can commit when your publisher asks you to get involved in promoting your book, posting on social media, or gathering followers' information. Do you have a full-time job?

Are you retired? The time investment to promote your book will be the same either way. There is a direct correlation between the success of a book and the involvement of the author in the promotion of that book.

WHY THIS BOOK WILL SAVE YOU FRUSTRATION AND TIME

This book will serve as Publishing Options 101. While the main components of most channels to publish are revealed, they only scratch the surface of the intricacies of the publishing industry. The information included in this book is meant as a reference for all publishing types and to provide some real questions for vetting potential publishers. You will learn the basic differences between all types of publishing and gain enough knowledge to dialogue with publishers without being blind-sided by publishing-ese.

The goal of this book is to guide you through the sometimes confusing process of publishing and save you time and frustration by avoiding potential issues you may not even be aware exist.

CHAPTER 1

GOALS

Goals. We set them in all areas of our lives, and when publishing a book, it's no different.

There are obvious scheduling goals for your book, but it is also wise to think of the big picture. You've worked hard. Dream a little, it feels good. But remember to set some realistic goals as well to ensure a good publishing experience.

"WHY"

One of the biggest questions I ask potential authors is, "When the reader is finished with your book, what is the main idea or thought you want to leave them with?" While this may sound like a no-brainer, it makes the author pause a moment to think of their "why". The "why" means, why are you writing this book? To help, to educate, to entertain, to document events? No matter what "the why", figuring it out before, during, and/or after you've written the book will help narrow down the focus of the book and help target the audience which will help in marketing your book later on.

Additionally, this question makes the author think like a reader for a moment, something writers tend to forget their focus of writing the book. What do readers' opinions matter when choosing a publisher? Readers buy your books, and one of the publisher's goals is to sell your book. If you don't think about this now, whoever you submit the book to will so it's a good idea to be prepared.

After establishing the reason you wrote the book and who you envision your audience to be, it helps to have a short elevator pitch ready when talking with potential publishers. Think of this pitch as a short two to three-minute speech with an emphasis on the book's highlights.

An example of this type of pitch is:

My personal journey through ten years of misdiagnosis only to find out my environment was making me physically and mentally ill. People need to know the dangers that lurk in and outside the average US home. I provide many personal examples and cite scientific evidence behind my findings. I am well today only because of my perseverance to get healthy. Helping others navigate potential issues is now my main focus, so they can hopefully avoid illness or have possible causes for healthcare providers when nothing has worked before.

SALES

All authors want to sell books. Whether to break even from a financial investment or to ensure a comfy retirement, selling a lot of books is a logical goal. However, a word of advice when setting sales goals; you get what you put in.

Again the two main investments that are tied to your sales goals are time and money. Unless you have friends in high places, you will be spending time promoting, and more often than not, you will also be investing financially in the marketing of your book.

PLATFORM

Platform is a word you will hear from every publisher, and it contains two main components. The first component is comprised of several questions: What do you stand for? What is the book about? Does the book speak to a group of people or an organization? The second component consists of your followers, your fans, and your support system.

Both components work together to create your base for guaranteed sales. The more relatable and topical your book is, together with a large existing following, makes it very appealing to publishers. These two things show that your book is marketable. The more marketable a book, the better the experience you will likely have with your publisher.

CHAPTER 2

OVERVIEW OF ALL TYPES OF PUBLISHING

This chapter will touch on the basic forms of book publishing. Each main publishing path will be featured in more detail in a separate chapter.

The traditional publishing model in a nutshell is based on the publisher taking on the financial risk of publishing, and the author is given an advance upfront.

Independent publishers may use the traditional model or some form of author financial investment. The amount of investment and level of publisher involvement varies with each publisher.

THE BIG FIVE

The Big Five is commonly known as the ultimate, brass ring of book publishing. Big Five publishers are Penguin Random House, HarperCollins, Hachette, Simon & Schuster, and Macmillan, all of which have many offshoot imprints dedicated to many genres. These publishers are known for bringing in the highest sales revenue books in the industry, the widest worldwide distribution, and the largest advances to authors.

The Big Five use the traditional publishing model (more on that in a later chapter) though they also are expanding into the hybrid publishing space as well.

ACADEMIC/UNIVERSITY/SMALL PRESSES

Though not a part of The Big Five, Academic publishers also follow the traditional publishing model and publish textbooks and educational books. Houghton Mifflin Harcourt, Scholastic, Sourcebooks, and W.W. Norton are a few examples in this category.

University Presses are specifically focused on publishing academic and scholarly journals and are associated with specific universities. They operate on the traditional model.

Small Presses, while many follow the traditional model, have fewer amenities compared to Academic and University presses. More on that in a bit.

INDEPENDENT PUBLISHERS

As mentioned before, independent publishers can use a traditional or hybrid (author-financed) model.

Some classify Independent publishers as every other publisher outside of The Big Five, whether or not they use the traditional or author-paid model.

The breakdown of Independent Publishers is primarily based on the following three business models:

TRADITIONAL

The author provides no upfront capital to the publisher to publish their book. There may or may not be an advance paid to the author.

HYBRID

The publisher chooses what is published. Authors provide capital along with the publisher's investment to cover publishing costs and marketing of the book. Costs vary depending on the level of partnership and services.

SERVICE PROVIDER

The company provides all the services to publish for a fee. Marketing is sometimes added as an additional cost option. The publisher has no investment in the book. (This option has also been called a Vanity Press.)

SELF-PUBLISHING / AUTHOR-PUBLISHED

While the industry has called this option self-publishing since its formation, with the increase in quality of the books being published without a publisher or services provider, this option is gradually becoming known as author-published. The movement to the new name helps break the stigma that the publishing industry has long put on the term "self-published".

As the name suggests, the author handles all aspects of publishing and marketing their books. While they may hire outside services to help, they serve as their own publishing company.

CHAPTER 3

THE BIG FIVE

As previously mentioned, the Big Five publishers are Penguin Random House, HarperCollins, Hachette, Simon & Schuster, and Macmillan.

In addition to using the traditional publishing model, the following are more aspects that distinguish them from other publishing models.

Note: The author may or may not own the copyright to the published work.

ADVANCE

The Big Five publishing houses will pay the authors an advance upfront to publish their book. The advance amount will depend on several factors such as: author following, genre, series potential, sales projections, release schedule, and publisher imprint. Advances generally are $5,000-10,000 for first-time authors.

ROYALTIES

Royalties are paid to the author when the advance earns out. Meaning once the publisher makes back their investment (the advance), the author will start earning royalties at usually around 15% (this will vary based on the deal).

DISTRIBUTION

Distribution is global, with a sales force that contacts bookstores directly. These presses use traditional distribution where books are printed in advance, warehoused, and orders are fulfilled for retailers, online, or wholesale distributors.

COSTS

The author pays no upfront costs to the publisher in a Big Five deal.

PROS & CONS

PROS
- No upfront cost
- Global distribution
- Established expertise
- Sales force
- Notoriety
- Prestige
- Media coverage/reviews
- Top book editors

CONS
- Need an agent to pitch the book to publishers
- Finding and working a deal with agent
- Most authors do not see royalties after advance
- Sales expectations must be made or exceeded
- Publisher holds rights indefinitely

- Little creative control over cover design
- Author must help in promoting the book

CHAPTER 4

ACADEMIC/UNIVERSITY PRESSES

Books focused on education, and niche genres like poetry and children's are good candidates for these types of presses.

Wiley, Tynsdale, Chronicle, and Kensington are a few more examples of academic presses in addition to the previous list for this category.

There are approximately 125 University Presses in the United States.

Note: The author may or may not own the copyright to the published work.

ADVANCE

Academic presses may pay authors an advance upfront to publish their book, however, the amount varies greatly and is usually less than those offered by The Big Five.

University presses rarely pay advances on projects.

ROYALTIES

Academic and University presses will immediately pay royalties if there is no advance. If there were a modest advance, it would have to earn out before royalties are paid.

DISTRIBUTION

Academic presses either use a traditional distributor (books print in advance) or have a sales force for sell-in to retailers and libraries/schools.

University presses have distribution but rarely have an extensive sales force.

Most of these presses use traditional distribution similar to The Big Five.

COSTS

There are no upfront costs paid by the author to the publisher.

PROS & CONS

PROS
- No upfront cost
- Niche categories
- Expertise of entire company
- No agent needed in most cases
- Notoriety & prestige
- Media coverage/reviews
- Editor is provided

CONS
- Smaller advances
- Library focused sell-in
- Very selective acquisitions
- Authors may have little say in the cover design
- Author must help in promoting the book

CHAPTER 5

INDEPENDENT PUBLISHERS

There are over 2,000 independent publishers in the United States as of 2023, so choosing the right one can be confusing. Having your goals and the questions in Chapter 7 handy when interviewing potential publisher partners, will help you make the right choice.

While there are many sites that watchdog the quality of independent publishers, a good resource to consult is the Independent Book Publishers Association (IBPA).

Note: The author always owns the copyright to their book.

TRADITIONAL

ADVANCE

There may or may not be a small advance paid to authors by independent traditional publishers.

ROYALTIES

Royalty rates are paid once the author has earned out any advance or royalties will be paid immediately if no advance has been paid to the author. Royalty rates vary, and some publishers may create a sliding royalty rate that increases for the author as the sales increase.

DISTRIBUTION

Distribution is usually global and can be either traditional or print-on-demand. Reminder: traditional distribution is when books are printed in advance and warehoused for fulfillment to retailers or wholesalers; print-on-demand is when orders are printed and fulfilled as orders are placed.

Global distribution with a company like Ingram Wholesale is also an option using the print-on-demand option again saving the advance printing overhead cost.

COSTS

There are no upfront costs paid by the author to the publisher.

PROS & CONS

PROS
- No upfront cost
- Global distribution
- Smaller publisher team
- Usually, no agent is needed
- May increase royalties as sales increase
- Edit is provided

CONS
- May require an agent pitch or proposal
- Small, if any, advance
- Authors may have little say in the cover design
- Author must help in promoting the book

HYBRID

Hybrid publishers vet manuscript submissions for quality or for content that fits the publisher's mission and goals.

Both author and publisher invest monies in the publishing of the author's book. While the author may initially put in the majority of the funds, the publisher and author are partners in promoting the book for the duration of the publishing agreement.

Note: The author always owns the copyright.

ADVANCE

There are no advances in a hybrid publishing agreement.

ROYALTIES

Royalty plans vary among hybrid publishers. Most offer 50%-100% of net royalties. Some provide sliding royalty scales that increase as higher sales goals are met.

DISTRIBUTION

While some hybrid publishers have traditional distribution with larger distribution companies and print advance copies for the sales team, most utilize a global distribution company that uses print-on-demand to fulfill orders.

Examples of print-on-demand companies include Ingram Wholesale (IngramSpark and Lightning Source) and KDP.

COSTS

Costs vary based on what the publisher provides. Packages range from $5,000-$30,000+.

It is important to ask what exactly you are getting in the package. A reputable publisher will be completely transparent with what they provide and don't provide.

PROS & CONS

PROS
- Professionally published
- Published under publisher imprint
- Flexible packages
- Experts in publishing
- Partnership with publisher
- Books are easily updated

CONS
- Upfront cost
- Marketing is usually an additional cost
- Books are rarely stocked in brick-and-mortar stores
- Author must help in promoting the book
- Editor may be extra expense
- Print-on-demand costs cut into royalties

SERVICE PROVIDER

Service providers do not vet submitted books but publish most all books submitted.

Examples of service providers are BookBaby and Lulu.

Note: The author owns the copyright.

ADVANCE

There are no advances in a service provider publishing agreement.

ROYALTIES

Authors receive 100% of the net royalties.

DISTRIBUTION

While some service providers have traditional distribution with larger distribution companies and print advance copies, most utilize print-on-demand to fulfill orders after the initial release.

COSTS

Costs vary based on what the service provider offers. Packages range from $1,500-$5,000+

It is important to ask what exactly you are getting in the package. A reputable service provider will be completely transparent with what they provide and don't provide.

PROS & CONS

PROS
- Printed book
- Lower cost
- Flexible packages
- Cover & layout designed
- Marketing packages available

CONS

- Upfront cost
- Author must do book promotion
- Marketing is extra
- Focus on package sales *not* book sales
- May require larger print order in advance
- Editing is an extra cost

CHAPTER 6

SELF-PUBLISHING / AUTHOR-PUBLISHED

Author-published (self-published) is the publishing option where you have total control over the whole process.

The author hires all the professionals to produce the highest quality book they can. Editors, proofreaders, designers, and marketing experts are examples of some of the contractors the author may need to hire.

Companies specializing in the services needed to author-publish include but are not limited to Reedsy, Fiver, UpWork, Bowker, KDP, and IngramSpark.

ADVANCE

There are no advances when the author publishes a book on their own.

ROYALTIES

The author retains 100% of all royalties in all formats that are published.

DISTRIBUTION

The most cost-effective way to distribute an author-published book is through print-on-demand services with IngramSpark and/or KDP. While the per unit cost may cut into the final royalty, it is usually far less than printing a large quantity, finding a company to warehouse, and fulfilling/shipping orders by yourself.

COSTS

If the author can produce a high-quality book with no help, the only costs incurred will come from the marketing of the book.

At the very minimum, most authors need to hire an editor, proofreader, and designer to create a professional and industry-standard book.

Many author-publishers realize early on that hiring professionals to help market the book is another cost but a good investment.

PROS & CONS

PROS
- Printed book
- Lower cost
- Total control of look
- Total control of schedule
- 100% of royalties

CONS
- No support
- Author does all book promotion

- Marketing is up to the author
- Quality can be less than industry-standard
- Author edits and proofreads
- Author sets up all distribution accounts
- Author uploads all files to distribution sites

CHAPTER 7

VETTING YOUR FUTURE PUBLISHER

OK, you now have a grasp on the main options for publishing your book. So what now? Now the fun begins! You get to interview your potential publisher!

Let me preface this by saying that some of these questions are targeted toward independent publishers not The Big Five, but if you get the Golden Ticket to one of those publishers, you still need to ask questions.

I can tell you, personally, I am hearing about more authors turning down Big Five offers to pursue independent publishing options because of a more flexible business model and potential to earn more in royalties.

Again, this goes back to knowing what your goals are. If being an author in one of The Big Five's catalogs with all the potential media and fame that could offer is best for you; go for it! If helping people heal or gain inspiration through your story and sales are just a secondary bonus and you author-publish; go for that! It really doesn't matter which option you choose as long as it fits your goals and you do due diligence to know all your options.

EXPECTATIONS & PARTNERSHIP BETWEEN AUTHOR AND PUBLISHER

It is very important to point out that communicating of shared expectations between you, the author, and your publisher will help ensure the best possible experience in publishing your book. Make sure you establish from the beginning that you will be proactive in communicating with your publisher, agent, or acquiring editor. Remember that even though you and your book are special, it is preferable for you to contact the publisher with questions, rather than for them to anticipate what you are thinking.

There are many stories out there about bad experiences from both authors and publishers. Without knowing both sides, my observation has been that if more time had been spent on focused communication, the experience could have been more pleasant for all parties. That focus comes from transparency by the publisher and the author researching options and asking questions before any agreement is signed.

COPYRIGHT

Never let anyone, except you, own the copyright to your story! If the publisher's agreement states they own the copyright, fight for your right to change this. If you budge on this because it is your dream publisher, know there may be consequences down the road.

For example, the publisher may put out a second edition with parts that are rewritten or added, and depending on your deal, you may or may not have any say in these revisions because you do not own the copyright to the book, the publisher does.

TIMELINE

Depending on the publisher you choose, you will find there are many differences in the amount of time it takes to publish a book.

The Big Five can take one-and-a-half to two years or more to publish your work. Academic, University and Small Presses can take up to two years.

On the independent side, timelines can be shorter, but the traditional independent publishers will oftentimes take a bit longer because of timing with their distributor's sales force.

Hybrid books usually take between four months to one year depending on their release schedule and if there is a strategic marketing plan attached.

Service Providers range from days to months depending on the package and services they provide. If the book is ready to publish (print-ready PDFs) it can take a few days, but if you need editing, proofreading, and design, it can take a couple months.

Author-publishing timelines are completely up to you and your schedule.

ROYALTIES

When talking with the publisher about your royalty share, ask them to explain in detail how the amount is derived.

For example, the publisher may say you will receive 75% royalty per book. So when a book sells for $18.99, that's $14.25.

Not too shabby, right? Well, not exactly, most deals will base the royalty percentage on the net profit of the book.

Net profit is based on the retail price minus the costs incurred to print and distribute the book which depending on the length and size of the book can be anywhere from 60-70% of that cost.

If the rate is 63% of retail then instead of making $14.25 on the $18.99 book, the net profit is now around $7.00 if you make 100% of your net profit. If you have to split that with your publisher, your royalty amount will be even less.

You may choose to ask if there is a possibility of a sliding royalty scale with the percentage of your royalties increasing at certain sales milestones.

Make sure when vetting your publisher you find out not only *how much* you will be getting for your royalty but also *when* you will be paid. Some publishers pay once a year, some twice a year, some pay quarterly.

No matter when they pay, make sure you understand that most distributors are at least ninety days behind in reporting sales to accommodate any returns that may come in. Remember how I said in the beginning how publishing is a slow process, this part probably is the hardest to accept because of the time lag.

Also, if your distributor receives returns after those ninety days, know that most publishers will deduct that from the next royalty report if you have been paid already for the sale of the books that were now returned.

LICENSING AND RIGHTS - AUDIO, EBOOK, TV/MOVIE RIGHTS, NFTS

This section ranks right up with copyright ownership in my opinion. Licensing and rights are very important and sometimes glanced over in publishing agreements. Make sure you understand the parameters around the agreement and if you want to give rights other than only the publishing of the book to your publisher.

What does this mean? When you enter your publishing agreement, it's pretty standard for the publisher to have rights to publish all formats of the book like audio, hardcover, paperback, and eBook. However, as more books are garnering attention from entertainment and production companies, film and television rights are being added to agreements between publishers and authors.

You may ask yourself why a publisher would ask for a share of the licensing of movie or television rights. It's quite simple; if the publisher hadn't published the book, chances are, the story wouldn't have had the credibility or visibility to be considered by the entertainment industry.

MARKETING & PR

Marketing and PR (public relations) are very important for the success of your book but are rarely included in the basic publishing packages by Hybrid Publishers and Service Providers. However, marketing and PR are included when working with a traditional publisher, whether one of The Big Five or an independent traditional publisher.

I will note here that even if you are publishing with one of The Big Five publishers, you should definitely ask exactly what they will be doing to market your book. Their answer may be: "We have a team". If so, please respond with, "Fantastic! I'd love to know what I can do to cross-promote what they are doing. Can you give me a schedule and grid of their plan?"

I guarantee that once the shock wears off, they will really appreciate the proactive attitude.

When it comes to marketing and PR with Hybrids and service providers, make sure you get a listing of the costs and a description of what is offered. Also, ask if they are open to suggestions from you for marketing and PR opportunities.

For example, I have authors who are experts in their fields and are heavily involved in certain groups and associations. They know their audience better than I do and since we are partners in the publishing process, I welcome their ideas to utilize their existing relationships for greater reach and press. This is the advantage of seeing the relationship between authors and publishers as a partnership.

Also, make sure the budget is defined as to what costs the publisher will cover and what costs the author is responsible for. If you use a hybrid or service provider, ask about payment plans and options for adding more services later.

One bit of advice no matter whom you publish with; don't go rogue. Marketing and PR are best when supported by the whole team, author, publisher, and all who support the project with a focused, cohesive, coordinated campaign. Don't mix your messages, but do create focused messaging for each market and media outlet.

CHAPTER 8

OTHER ASPECTS OF BOOK PUBLISHING

Remember in the Author-published section where those possible extra costs were listed? Here are some estimates of what you can expect to pay for professionals in these areas.

BOOK COACHES

What is a book coach? A book coach is someone who will guide you through concepting, developing, and writing your story, choosing the right kind of editor at the right time, helping you find the right designers and even helping you find a publisher that fits your story and goals.

Pricing ranges from hourly (some starting at $50 per hour) to monthly retainers of several thousand dollars.

Like all aspects of publishing your book, do your research, ask the questions, and find the coach who is a good fit for you, your budget, and your book.

EDITORS

In my opinion, finding a good editor who can keep your voice while helping craft a better book can be one of the hardest tasks aside from actually writing the book. One of the most reputable sites to find a good editor is Reedsy.com.

PROOFREADERS

Fun fact, most copy editors are not paying attention to spelling. You will need a proofreader. Again, check out Reedsy or hire an English-major student if you are on a budget.

BOOK COVER DESIGN

We've all heard that you aren't supposed to judge a book by its cover but that saying is NOT actually talking about book covers, it's talking about not judging people. When it comes to book covers, there are many wonderful designers out there that WANT you to judge it and even NEED you to judge that book by the cover to stay in business.

A good professional cover is key, especially in a market where many sales are done online by a small thumbnail view. It's not just about a pretty picture, in fact, the most important thing on that cover is the typefaces used. The type must be more than legible; it needs to fit the genre, be spaced and sized correctly (kerning and leading), and basically just really stand out.

While Canva is making cover design easy, it doesn't mean they are good. Though, with guidance, you can make a nice cover that can do the job. Many authors now use 99designs and Fiver when they are self-publishing.

If you have the budget, hire a professional designer to help you. You will never regret a great cover that is the face of your book. You can expect to pay from $300-3000 for a cover design (this cost may include the back cover and spine as well if needed).

No matter which direction you decide to go for cover design, it is advised to always get feedback from others. As a former professor, I always told my students: "Just because you can, doesn't mean you should" followed shortly by, "I can't teach you taste." Art is subjective, but book cover design is more than art, it is the first impression of your book.

MARKETING, PUBLICITY & REVIEWS OH MY!

Remember the saying earlier; you get back what you put in? Here is where it pays off the most. Of course, putting together a professional-looking and well-written book is key for having a product to sell, it's in the promotion where everything literally pays off.

Get active on your personal website and if you don't have one, get one. All it takes is a couple of pages or a scrolling page. Key things to include on your site: your bio, book cover, book description/synopsis, link to a sales page for the book, blog (optional), and contact form to gain a follower list.

Pro-tip regarding follower lists: utilize that list to offer pages from the "edit floor" and let them know when you have appearances or even bounce new book ideas off them. They truly want to hear from you. You are their author-celebrity.

I would be remiss if I did not mention social media. Before you wave it off, think of it as free advertising and a way to connect to reviewers, readers, and most of all, buyers. Start slow, pick one. I suggest Instagram so you can post pics and longer posts to reach larger audiences. That said, if you already have a following on another outlet, use it.

Reviews are key, so build your following and ask for reviews. Don't be surprised when friends and family "keep forgetting" to leave a review. You will have a new respect for the strangers that pick up your book and leave a review.

Keep your eyes and ears open for opportunities to be a guest on a podcast or start your own. If you do start your own, know that consistency is key in building an audience there too; this is a big time commitment.

ASSOCIATIONS & NETWORKING

I mentioned them before and I will again, if you are publishing with an independent publisher or author-publish, you'll want to join the Independent Book Publishers Association (IBPA). The resources and networking alone are worth the application fee, but the friendships and knowledge you will gain when you get involved are priceless.

Depending on the genre you are writing in, there are usually local writing groups that are great connections. For example, Sister in Crime, ThrillerFest, Camp NaNoWriMo, Chronicles, or just search Facebook for all types of writing and publishing groups.

Another great way to network is to check out in-person events like book festivals. Tucson Festival of Books in March, LA Times Book Festival in April, Printer's Row Lit Fest in Chicago in September, and Miami Book Fest in November are several of the largest in the country and bring in authors, publishers, and readers of all types of books.

Also, look for workshops and conferences online and in person like Publish with Purpose, Women in Publishing, PubU, ABA Winter Institute, U.S. Book Show, and the ALA Annual Conference.

CHAPTER 9

FINAL THOUGHTS

So based on your goals, what did you decide? I actually hope you haven't made a definitive decision until you interview at least one publisher in the traditional, hybrid, and service provider space. I also hope you dig deeper into the author-published option.

Be honest with yourself and be honest with the publishers you talk to. No one wants to waste anyone's time or money. For those of us who are truly passionate about publishing good books and educating writers about their options to become published authors, we welcome inquisitions.

Nothing makes me happier than speaking with a writer that knows a bit about their options but is open to learning about out-of-the-box ways to publish and market their book.

WHEN AM I DONE?

OK, OK, OK. I know by this time, you are probably thinking, this isn't so hard, I need to start googling, and you'd be right. I gave you the business models of your publishing options, it's going to be a wonderful rabbit hole of information once you start looking into each option.

Oh, and when will you be done with this first book? Probably when you are repeating the process for your next one.

Publishing is the long game; it's an exercise in patience. Don't give up on your first book after your eighth book.

My wish for you is to choose the right words and find the best publisher for your needs.

Good Luck!

RESOURCES

THE BIG FIVE

Hachette Book Group
https://www.hachettebookgroup.com/

Simon & Schuster
https://www.simonandschuster.com/

Penguin Random House
https://www.penguinrandomhouse.com/

HarperCollins
https://www.harpercollins.com/

Macmillan
https://us.macmillan.com/

ASSOCIATIONS / NETWORKING / WORKSHOPS

Independent Book Publishers Association (IBPA)
https://www.ibpa-online.org/

Women in Publishing
https://womeninpublishingsummit.com/

Publish with Purpose
http://publishwithpurposesummit.com/

IBPA PubU
https://www.publishinguniversity.org/

CONTRACTORS

Reedsy https://reedsy.com

Fiverr https://www.fiverr.com/

UpWork https://www.upwork.com/

Canva https://www.canva.com/

FESTIVALS

Tucson Festival of Books
https://tucsonfestivalofbooks.org/

Printers Row Lit Fest - Chicago
http://printersrowlitfest.org/

LA Times Festival of Books
https://events.latimes.com/festivalofbooks/

Miami Book Fair

https://www.miamibookfair.com/

Southern Festival of Books - Nashville https://sofestof-books.org/

ACKNOWLEDGMENTS

A big thank you to Pony Jean Parker, who was the inspiration for the title of this book with her "OMG! I WROTE A BOOK" cake at her book release party.

A huge thank you to my amazing friends who have been supportive of my publishing company and, finally now, in writing my first book.

To Dennis, I couldn't have created this business and kept pursuing my dreams without your support. Thank you for putting up with it all.

To my dad, thank you for instilling in me the drive to pursue my dreams. I know you're always with me. To my mom, thank you for supporting me even without understanding anything I was working on. You both have been the backbone of who I am.

Everyone who has been in and out of my life, you all had a purpose, and I thank you.

There always has to be a first, and this is mine. *Enjoy.*

ABOUT THE AUTHOR

From an early age, JuLee Brand always wanted to create things. Book covers and type inspired her to pursue a career in design. After several years as Production Manager for Reunion Records, she moved to High Five Entertainment and designed television motion graphics for series, award shows, and specials.

In 2010, after receiving her MFA from Full Sail University, she began teaching part-time at colleges, universities, and design schools while also working full-time designing television and print graphics.

But it was her move to Hachette Book Group Nashville as Art Director in 2012 where JuLee learned the workings of the publishing world behind the curtain. Art Directing and designing book covers for Joyce Meyer, Lauraine Snelling, Karen Kingsbury, Brian D. McLaren, Julissa Arce, and Nadia Bolz-Weber to name a few.

Everyone has a story, and that inspiration sparked the creation of W. Brand Publishing in 2018. Along with the goal of publishing great books and designing attention-grabbing covers, Brand hopes the authors' stories provide enlightenment, entertainment, and connection to the reader. Her mantra, words matter, has now become part of her brand and mission.

JuLee also writes both fiction and non-fiction books in her spare time and is a board member of the Independent Book Publishers Association (IBPA) and serves on the Hybrid Criteria Committee and Advocacy Committee.

She lives in Nashville, where her floofy co-workers create major traffic jams to the coffee maker every morning. When JuLee isn't working, she loves a glass of full-bodied red wine and traveling to new places with fantastic food and amazing views. She strives to live in gratitude every day.

https://www.wbrandpub.com/
https://www.designchik.net/
Facebook and Instagram: @wbrandpub

Made in the USA
Middletown, DE
24 February 2023